Contents

📖 Fiction

🔍 Non-fiction

Written by
Dennis Hamley

Illustrated by
Mark Boardman

Series editor **Dee Reid**

Heinemann

Part of Pearson

Characters

Zarek

Pilot,
Ben Jones

Tricky words

- competition
- fastened
- turbulence
- height
- violently
- terrified
- response
- calm

Read these words to the student. Help them with these words when they appear in the text.

Introduction

Zarek had won a competition to fly with Ben, an RAF pilot, in a two-seater Hawk trainer. They took off, but suddenly the plane started shaking. Ben thought it was just turbulence, but then the plane began to shake violently and smoke poured out of the engine. Ben was knocked out. Zarek used the radio to call for help.

Remote Control

Zarek had won a competition.
He was going to fly with an RAF pilot.
He would be flying in a two-seater Hawk trainer.
Same plane as the Red Arrows,
thought Zarek. *Cool!*

"Hi," said the pilot. "I'm Flying Officer Ben Jones. Ready for take-off?"
Zarek climbed into the plane and fastened his belt. The plane sped along the runway and took off.

Suddenly, the plane started shaking.
"What is going on?" cried Zarek.

"Just a bit of turbulence," said Ben.
"Don't worry."
Then the plane started to lose height.
Zarek was scared.

The plane was shaking violently.
"This turbulence is getting worse," said Ben.
Zarek was really scared.
Then he heard Ben shout, "The engine has failed! I can't hold it!"
Zarek saw Ben press the engine restart button.
Nothing happened.

Bang!
Zarek looked out of his window.
Smoke was pouring from the engine!

Zarek looked at Ben. The bang had made him hit his head against the window.
He was knocked out!

Zarek was terrified.
He shook Ben.
"Wake up! Wake up!" he shouted.
There was no response.

The plane was out of control.
It was nose-diving towards the ground.
It was going to crash!
If I don't do something quickly, we're going to die! thought Zarek.

Then he had an idea.
He leaned over and took the pilot's radio.
"Help! Help!" he shouted into the radio.
"We're going to crash!"

There was no response.
The radio was dead.
Then Zarek heard a crackle and a voice said:
"This is Flying Officer Adam Reed.
Don't worry. I'm going to guide you in."

"The engine has failed!" cried Zarek. "And the pilot's been knocked out. I can't fly the plane!"
"Calm down and take hold of the controls," said Adam.
His voice was calm.
"There is a button in front of you marked 'engine restart' – press it."

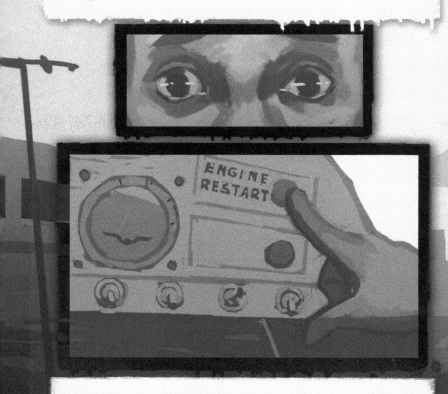

"It won't work," said Zarek.
But it did.
Zarek suddenly felt calm.
Somehow, everything seemed under control.

"I'm going to take over the controls," said Adam.
"The plane is fitted with a remote control system.
I can fly it from the control tower."
Zarek felt the plane change direction.
"I'm going to guide the plane on to the
runway," said Adam. "Just stay calm."

The ground was getting closer.
"Stay calm," Zarek said to himself.
"Adam can land this plane."
He held his breath.
The plane hit the runway.
It shook violently but it did not crash.

The plane came to a stop.
The ground crew came running over.
They helped Zarek out of the plane
and called an ambulance for Ben.

"How did you manage to land?" asked one of them.
Zarek told them what had happened.
"Flying Officer Adam Reed guided me in," he said.
"We would have crashed without him."

The ground crew looked shocked.
"That's not possible," said one of them.
"We lost radio contact with you just after take-off."
"And you couldn't have spoken to Flying Officer
Adam Reed," said another man. "He was
in an accident last week. He lost control of his
plane and it crashed. He was killed."

Literal comprehension

p5 What did Ben think was the problem at first?

p16 Why were the ground crew shocked at Zarek's account?

Inferential comprehension

p3 How can we tell Zarek was excited about winning the competition?

p12 Why did Zarek say the restart button wouldn't work?

p12 Why did Zarek feel everything was under control?

Personal response

- How do you think the plane landed safely?
- Do you think Zarek will be put off flying ever again?

Word knowledge

p6 Find an adverb.

p8 Find a word that means 'very scared'.

p15 Find four past tense verbs ending 'ed'.

Spelling challenge

Read these words:

shouted   making   worked

Now try to spell them!

Ha! Ha! Ha!

Why do birds fly south?

Because it's too far to walk!

Find out about

- when plane engines stop working and the pilots have to land in pretty dangerous conditions.

Tricky words

- machines
- powerful
- dangerous
- volcano
- erupts
- passengers
- rescued
- seriously

Read these words to the student. Help them with these words when they appear in the text.

Introduction

Planes are amazing machines. Their engines are big and powerful. Sometimes things go wrong and engines can stop working mid-air. If the engines aren't restarted quickly, the plane will crash. Sometimes ash from a volcano or a flock of birds can make the engines stop working.

Miracle Landings

BRITISH AIRWAYS

Planes are amazing machines!
Their engines are much bigger and more powerful
than 100 Formula 1 car engines put together.
They can fly at over 30,000 feet above the ground
and they can reach speeds of over 500mph.

Plane engines hardly ever stop working.
But sometimes things can go wrong.
Engines can stop working in mid-air.
This is very dangerous.
If the engines aren't restarted quickly,
the plane will crash.

What makes an engine stop working?

Lots of things can stop an engine working.
Sometimes a volcano erupts.
Ash flies up into the sky.
It can get inside a plane's engines and
make them stop working.

Ash got inside the engines of a plane flying from Hong Kong to Australia.

All four engines on the jumbo jet stopped working. It looked as though the plane would crash and everyone on it would die.

But the crew got the engines to start again. The plane reached Australia safely.

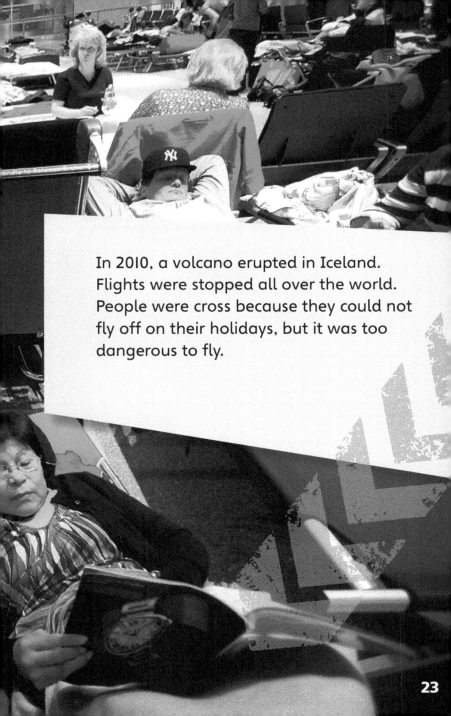

In 2010, a volcano erupted in Iceland. Flights were stopped all over the world. People were cross because they could not fly off on their holidays, but it was too dangerous to fly.

Birds

Sometimes birds can make an engine fail.
They get sucked into the engine and stop
it working.
This happened to a plane in the USA.
On 16th January 2010, a US Airways plane
took off from an airport in New York.
It flew straight into a flock of birds.

Both engines stopped working.
The pilot knew that the plane would
not make it back to the airport.
He had to think quickly what to do.
He decided to land the plane in the
Hudson River.

Landing on water is very dangerous.
If the pilot had made any mistakes, the plane
could have hit the water and smashed into
pieces, killing all the passengers.

Luckily, the pilot was very skilful and he did not make any mistakes.

He landed safely on the river.

All 155 passengers were rescued before the plane sank.

Nobody was killed.

Fuel

Sometimes the engines stop working because there is a problem with the fuel. This happened to a plane as it came in to land at London's Heathrow airport in 2008. As the pilot was getting ready to land, all the engines stopped working.

The plane was coming down very quickly.
It just missed crashing on to a road next to
the airport. It passed just 6 metres above
the busy traffic. The plane landed on the
grass 300 metres short of the runway.
All 136 passengers were safely rescued.
Just one passenger was seriously injured.

When the plane was checked later it was found that ice had formed in the fuel tank. The ice had stopped the fuel reaching the engines and made them stop working.

Don't panic!

Most planes are very safe and their
engines are checked all the time.
There are millions of flights every year
all over the world and hardly any
crashes. In fact, you're more likely to
be killed by a bee sting than to be in a
plane crash!

Quiz

Text comprehension

Literal comprehension
p21 Why is an erupting volcano dangerous to a plane?
p25 Where did the US Airways pilot land?

Inferential comprehension
p19 Why is the title 'Miracle Landings'?
p19 Why do planes need powerful engines?
p31 Why should you not worry that the engines will
fail in a plane?

Personal response
• How do you think the passengers felt when all the engines
on the jumbo jet stopped working?
• Would you be nervous to fly in a plane?

Word knowledge

p23 Find two connectives in the third sentence.
p25 Find a word that means 'made up his mind'.
p29 Find two of the adjectives on this page.

Spelling challenge

Read these words:

everyone   above   please

Now try to spell them!

Ha! Ha! Ha!

Why did the pilot land his plane on a house?
Because the landing lights were on!